sport snaps

bert rosenthal

Michael Johnson

sprinter deluxe

This book is dedicated to my wife,
Emily, and my children, Gail, Scott,
Sandra and Rebecca.

B.R.

PHOTO CREDITS:

Allsport
Front Cover [M. Hewitt], 1 [R. Kinnaird],
3 [S. Botterill], 5 [M. Powell], 6 [M. Powell],
8 [M. Powell], 11 [A. Lyons], 12 [M. Powell],
13 [M. Powell], 14 [T. Duffy], 16 [M. Powell],
18 [M. Powell], 21 [T. Duffy], 22 [T. Duffy],
23 [M. Powell], 24 [G. Mortimore], 26 [M. Powell],
27 [Allsport], 28 [M. Powell], 30 [G. Mortimore],
31 [G. Mortimore], 32 [S. Bruty], 35 [A. Lyons],
36 [G. Mortimore], 38 [M. Powell], 41 [M. Cooper],
42 [G. Prior], 43 [J. Gichigi], 46 [A. Lyons],
47 [M. Powell], 49 [A. Lyons], 50 [A. Lyons],
54 [G. Prior], 56 [T. Duffy].

AP/Wide World
4, 7, 33, 45, 51.

Sun Media
52 [C. Robertson], 53 [C. Robertson].

Baylor University Athletic Media Relations
55 [P. Van Duievendyk].

Bert Rosenthal's photo courtesy of The Associated Press.

Printed by Pinnacle Press, Inc.
in the United States of America.

Edited by Carla Babrick.

Designed by Werremeyer|Floresca.

LIBRARY OF CONGRESS
CATALOG CARD NUMBER 00-107076

table of contents

the day

MICHAEL JOHNSON WILL NEVER FORGET

The scene was so uncharacteristic of Michael Johnson. Here he was, crossing the finish line of the 200 meters at the 1996 Olympics, and the usually stoic, serious-minded, thoughtful, introspective Johnson was acting like a man just given his freedom.

Johnson had just shattered his world record, not by the merest of margins but by .34 seconds – a vast decrease in so short an event.

So Johnson was ready to celebrate. He opened his mouth wide, thrust his arms out and up, as far apart as they would go, giving the impression he was ready to soar like an eagle, and he jumped up and down, indicating that he was ready for takeoff.

Then, after being given an American flag, he wrapped it around his broad shoulders and danced around the track in a victory lap before returning to the finish line area. With the clock on the field showing the time of 19.32 seconds, Johnson knelt down on the right side of the instrument panel and posed for pictures, his face lit with a tremendous sense of accomplishment.

The manner in which Johnson had flashed through the night on the lightning-fast Olympic Stadium track in Atlanta, his golden shoes glistening as his pistonlike

moves swiftly chewed up the surface, even left him stunned, along with his coach and one of his competitors.

Not only had he won the 200 in world record time, he had become the first man to sweep the 200 and 400 meters at the same Olympics.

"I had done something that few people ever get to do, to be the very best — the best ever! — at one thing," said Johnson. "I always wanted to bring the two events together in a way that nobody else had ever done. That sums up what my career is all about."

Coach Clyde Hart, who recruited Johnson for Baylor University in 1987, sat in the stands watching his remarkable protégé.

"After he passed the 100-meter mark, I looked at my stopwatch and saw the time," Hart said. "It was so much faster than ever before that I just clicked my watch off, sat back and enjoyed the rest of the race.

I didn't see the final time, and my assistant coach was hitting me and screaming, 'Look at the [official] time.' I did, and it still didn't register. I thought, 'That's not right. It'll switch back.' But it didn't."

Ato Boldon of Trinidad & Tobago, the 200-meter bronze medalist, also was in disbelief.

"I saw a blur go by, whoosh, and thought, 'There goes first,'" he said. "Nineteen thirty-two is not a time. It sounds like my dad's birth date."

Later in the interview room, Boldon said, "I had accepted the fact that the fastest man in the world was the winner of the 100 meters. Now I believe the fastest man alive is sitting to my left."

Sitting in the stands was an 81-year-old man who admittedly was "bawling like a baby." He was Fritz Pollard, who had been on the 1936 Olympic team with the great Jesse Owens, winner of four gold medals at the Berlin Games. As Pollard watched Johnson smash the record, the '36 bronze medalist in the 110-meter hurdles said, "That kid has got Jesse's spirit."

He had Jesse's talent, too.

MICHAEL JOHNSON profile

BORN:
SEPTEMBER 13, 1967.
DALLAS, TEXAS.

FAMILY:
WIFE, KERRY.
CHILD, SEBASTIAN.

FAVORITE FILMS: Mike Myers' Austin Powers movies and the Godfather series.

FAVORITE MUSICAL ARTISTS: Ray Charles and Aretha Franklin. He is a big music fan and is especially into R&B from the late 1960s and early 1970s.

HOBBY: Fishing. He only goes a few times a year, but he finds it "necessary time." It's quite a surprising diversion for Johnson, a man of speed, to enjoy fishing, an activity that requires a great deal of patience, a trait that is not one of Michael's assets.

FOR THE FILM ROLE OF MICHAEL JOHNSON: Cast Samuel L. Jackson. "He's unflappable," Michael said.

NICKNAMES: Because of his many achievements on the track, Johnson has been called "Superman" and "The REAL Magic Johnson."

BOOK: He already has written *Michael Johnson, Slaying the Dragon – How To Turn Your Small Steps into Great Feats.*

PRIZED POSSESSIONS: a Jesse Owens trading card he received for his birthday in 1996 from Owens' granddaughter and a letter from Owens' widow, Ruth, sent to him before the Atlanta Games. Ruth Owens said she saw her late husband in Johnson. "Greatest compliment I've ever been paid," Michael said.

For their first anniversary in 1999, Johnson's wife, Kerry, gave him an antique Australian gold pocket watch. He took it to Sydney for the 2000 Olympics as a good luck charm to bring home more gold.

SECOND CAREER: When his track career ends, Johnson might wind up in the broadcasting booth. He already has done commentary on some meets, enjoyed the experience and received high praise from his television partners and network executives. For example, NBC producer Sam Flood said Johnson has "unbelievable pipes" for TV. Those who have worked with him lauded his preparation for his assignments, and his succinct and straight-forward analysis.

COMMUNITY INVOLVEMENT: Johnson loves kids. He often visits camps and schedules autograph sessions for youngsters. He works with the Easter Seals program, serving as a spokesperson for the Dallas area, and for the Dallas public school system, frequently reading books to children and being a positive role model and mentor.

HEROES: First his parents, then Muhammad Ali and Jesse Owens. "There is so much I can learn from Muhammad Ali," Johnson said. "I can try to avoid his mistakes, to draw lessons from his victories, and to find inspiration in the fearless way he has lived his life. Like Jesse Owens, Ali has transcended sports."

"Owens ... courageously competed in the face of Adolf Hitler's racist tyranny in the 1936 Olympics in Berlin," Johnson added. "He was facing pressures that no other athlete will face again. In the center of a regime built on the myth of Aryan supremacy, Owens – who a year earlier had set six world records in one day – shattered the myth. ... Owens won four gold medals in the 1936 Games."

MICHAEL JOHNSON'S TRACK CAREER AND HIS WAY OF LIFE WERE LAID OUT FOR HIM EARLY. AS A YOUNGSTER, HE PLAYED A LOT OF SPORTS, BUT THERE WAS SOMETHING SPECIAL ABOUT MICHAEL. HE WAS THE FASTEST KID IN HIS NEIGHBORHOOD. WHEN THE BOYS CHALLENGED EACH OTHER TO RACES, JOHNSON ALWAYS WON. "I WAS ALWAYS THE FASTEST GUY," HE SAID.

MEDALS | Olympic and World Championship gold medals: 12

He didn't run because he envisioned being an Olympic sprinter. He ran because it was fun. He thrived on being the fastest. It's a natural reaction, whether you're a youth or an adult.

Michael began running for real at 10. He was matched against the fastest and strongest boys his age from parks throughout the city of Dallas in a 50-yard dash. When the starting gun went off, so did Michael. He ran faster than anyone, and as the winner, he was presented with a blue ribbon. He still remembers the exhilarating feeling of knowing that he was the fastest. He taps into that feeling every time he runs and every time he wins.

"He will be considered one of the greatest athletes in the Olympic movement."

JOHN CHAPLIN, COACH OF THE 2000 U.S. OLYMPIC MEN'S TRACK TEAM

Significantly, that competition was part of the Jesse Owens Games. Owens, the hero of the 1936 Olympics Games, later would loom large in Johnson's life.

At 11, Michael began running in summer meets and in junior high school. With his horned-rimmed glasses, the quiet Johnson looked more like a scholar than an athlete.

WORLD OUTDOOR RECORD | 300 meters: 31.85

31.85

That's just the way his parents, Paul Sr. and Ruby, wanted it. "Track didn't matter one way or the other with us," Ruby said.

"Education was everything," Paul said. "He just happened to run well, according to time."

Paul, a truck driver, and Ruby, a teacher, raised their five children – Michael was the youngest – to understand the significance of a good education. Michael's three sisters and his brother all graduated from North Texas University and fulfilled their father's hopes that "my kids are going to be something better than truck drivers." Michael's sisters and his brother all got their college degrees without the benefit of an athletic scholarship.

Michael proved to be the most academically gifted member of the family and wound up in Dallas' best high school, Skyline.

"In those days, my participation in track was a way
for me to get into a good college," Johnson said.
"But running never took precedence over my studies."

Neither did it take precedence over his father's philosophical teachings.

"We were told that if you start with everyone else, you'll end up with
everyone else," Paul Jr., Michael's brother, said. "We were taught, 'Don't
expect the norm. Go over and above what is expected.'"

"He was brought up in a home where his daddy taught him a lot,"
Johnson's coach, Clyde Hart, said. "Daddy was his role model.
Daddy would ask him how he intended to reach his goals. Michael
would tell him what his goals were, and his father would repeat
the question until he got the right answer. That stuck with him."

Michael's parents also were diligent, conscientious people who
planned everything out in a very orderly fashion. Johnson has
adapted those traits and perhaps taken them to extremes, but
he wants to be prepared for all situations. He once circled the
track at Baylor University alone in a storm, telling Coach Hart,
"You never know when you might have to run in the rain."

At Atwell Junior High, Johnson played football and ran track,
but he was not obsessed with sports like many youngsters of today.
In his first race there, he placed second in the 200, but he knew
he had to do well in the classroom, and he worked on being
a good student.

He didn't even run track in his first year at Skyline High because he wanted to concentrate on his studies. He long-jumped as a sophomore, then returned to running his junior year. Then he won some 200-meter races, but he was overshadowed in Dallas by Roy Martin, the nation's fastest schoolboy. Skyline coach Joel Ezer likened Michael's erect running style to that of "a statue."

"They say his feet never leave the ground," Ezer said, adding that the style "is very efficient."

Odd style or not, Johnson won the district 200-meter title as a senior, but he was beaten in the state championships by Derrick Florence, who would win the world junior 100-meter title that year.

Johnson's high school best for the 200 was 21.30, and he was not considered an outstanding college prospect.

"Nobody could predict how good he could be," said Hart, who recruited Johnson for Baylor University, hoping to use him on 1,600-meter relays, the Bears' specialty.

JOHNSON DECIDED ON BAYLOR BECAUSE THE FATHERLY HART STRESSED THAT AT THE SCHOOL HE WOULD RECEIVE A SOLID EDUCATION, JUST LIKE MICHAEL'S FAMILY WANTED, ALONG WITH A CHANCE TO COMPETE IN ATHLETICS. EDUCATION, THOUGH, WAS FIRST.

"IF ALL ATHLETES WERE TO GIVE SCHOOL AS MUCH OF THEIR CONCENTRATION AS DO POTENTIAL DOCTORS, LAWYERS OR BUSINESSMEN, THERE WOULDN'T BE ANY PROBLEMS FOR EX-STARS, WHO WERE CARELESS WITH THEIR STUDIES AND, AS A CONSEQUENCE, UNSUCCESSFUL IN LIFE AT THE CONCLUSION OF THEIR ACTIVE CAREERS," JOHNSON SAID.

AWARD | **1996 Sullivan Award, outstanding U.S. amateur athlete**

The chance to attend Baylor also would keep Johnson close to home, near his support team – his parents, brother and three sisters. Waco, Baylor's home, was less than 90 miles south of Dallas.

"Education was No. 1 with his family," Hart said. "His family made my job easier."

Hart saw something in Johnson that other recruiters didn't, and he was willing to offer Michael a scholarship. Johnson gladly accepted.

The coach was impressed by Johnson's abilities to focus, to establish a plan and to pursue it relentlessly – assets embedded in him by his father.

"I just felt he was going to develop and get better," Hart said. "And the way he ran reminded me of Jesse Owens."

Nobody worked harder in practice than Johnson. Nobody was as serious. Michael could be having fun one moment, then suddenly withdraw and go into a shell, off by himself, contemplating, thinking deeply.

"His 200 record is one of the greatest records of all. He's been very good for our sport. I've never heard him complain like a lot of other athletes. He's also trained with only one coach. When he reached success, he stayed with Coach [Clyde] Hart."

JIMMY CARNES, FORMER PRESIDENT OF USA TRACK & FIELD, AND NOW HEAD OF THE U.S. TRACK COACHES ASSOCIATION

"If you don't know him, you'd think he was angry," hurdler McClinton Neal, a friend, said, "but he's just thinking about what he needs to do. He's planning and he wants to be left alone. He can't be persuaded to be a certain way. He'll be himself from beginning to end."

Johnson liked his privacy and he didn't want to be disturbed. Some people called it aloofness. Johnson didn't care; he enjoyed being his own person. He lived life in his own way, and he ran in his own style. He was different, and there was nothing wrong with it. People tried changing his distinctive running style, and both Johnson and Hart scoffed at their suggestions. Why should they change? Not when Johnson was running so efficiently and effectively.

WORLD OUTDOOR RECORD | 1,600-meter relay: 2:54.20

"Foot placement is the key to speed," Hart said. "Many athletes place a foot slightly in front of their center of gravity and that actually causes a blocking effect. It's like they're putting on the brakes all the time."

Johnson ran in an erect position, his posture upright, with little knee lift and rapid turnover.

"While Michael may give up a little in stride length, he never stops moving," Hart said. "As one foot is hitting the track, the other is coming all the time and it forms nearly a complete circle. Also, Michael doesn't strain, which is often overlooked in running. Stride rate and stride length, with relaxation, is the ideal."

Track Tips for
Young Runners:
SETTING GOALS

MAKE YOUR GOALS REALISTIC AND REALIZE THAT YOU MIGHT NOT REACH A FEW OF THEM. "THE ABILITY TO SET REALISTIC GOALS ONLY COMES WITH EXPERIENCE AND WITH THE INTIMATE KNOWLEDGE OF YOURSELF THAT YOU ACQUIRE WHEN YOU'VE WORKED HARD AND TESTED YOURSELF," JOHNSON SAYS. "WHEN IN DOUBT, SCALE YOUR GOALS BACK A LITTLE. IF THE AIM IS REALISTIC, YOU'LL GET THERE SOON ENOUGH."

#2

The style perhaps could be compared to the steady beat of a metronome, but instead of swinging back and forth, Johnson churns steadily and rapidly along the track, faster than anyone at 200 and 400 meters.

Hart compares Michael's form to that of Jesse Owens, who not coincidentally is Johnson's track idol.

"If you put film of Michael and Jesse Owens next to each other, you can see the similarities," Hart said. "They almost look identical. It's very efficient."

" He didn't just break the record, he passed it by boundaries. He bypassed 19.6, 19.5, 19.4.

That's unbelievable."

CLYDE HART, JOHNSON'S COACH, AMAZED THAT MICHAEL COULD LOWER HIS 200-METER WORLD RECORD FROM 19.66 SECONDS TO 19.32 IN ONE RACE

Johnson wasted no time in showing the efficiency of his unusual style. In his first outdoor 200 for Baylor, he lost to Floyd Heard, one of the fastest 200 sprinters in the world at the time, by only one-tenth of a second. His time of 20.41 seconds was a school record.

"We had no idea he'd be that good," Hart said.

WORLD OUTDOOR RECORD | 400 meters: 43.18

Johnson's budding career was put on hold for a while when
he pulled a hamstring at the Drake Relays in April 1987. The injury
kept him out of the Southwest Conference Championships in May,
but he came back to post a 46.29 in his first 400, then ran a 45.2
leg on Baylor's 1,600-meter relay team that finished third at the
NCAA Championships in June.

Hart knew he had a potential star in his midst. The star glittered the following year. Johnson
opened his sophomore season with a 20.09 200 at the Texas A&M Relays April 16, and less
than an hour later, he ran a 44.00 anchor leg on the Bears' relay. A week later, he lowered his
400 personal best to 45.23 at the Baylor Invitational, and the next week at the Drake Relays,
he ripped off a 43.5 relay split. That blazing split prompted U.S. Olympic Coach Stan Huntsman
to say that he would take that lap, right then, as his anchor leg at the Seoul Games.

Johnson wasn't finished for the season
yet. In the Southwest Conference
Championships, he blazed a personal-best
20.07 200, finishing just behind eventual
Olympic gold medalist Joe DeLoach. Then,
injury struck again. This time, it was a
broken fibula, sustained during the
200 final at the NCAA Championships.
Johnson gamely attempted to run the
400 at the Olympic trials, but he limped
in last in his heat. Even so, his two fast
200 times earned him the No. 7 U.S.
ranking in that event for the year.

Track Tips for
Young Runners:
CHARTING GOALS

BE SPECIFIC. AT THE BEGINNING OF
A SEASON, CHART OUT YOUR PROGRAM
FOR THE YEAR, PINPOINTING THE DAY,
WEEK AND MONTH THAT YOU WANT TO
HIT SPECIFIC MARKS OR TIMES. THAT
TIGHTENS THE FOCUS ON YOUR DREAMS
AND TURNS THEM INTO GOALS.

#3

U.S. CHAMPION | five-time 200 meter champion

200

"I feel he has the ability to challenge world records at both the 200 and 400," Hart said.

Michael's junior year again began in promising fashion. He finished second to Antonio McKay in the 400 at the USA Indoor Championships. Then at the NCAA Indoor Championships at Indianapolis, he shattered the American record in the 200 – just as his coach had predicted – with 20.59 and led off Baylor's 1,600 relay with a 45.65 leg, faster than the collegiate 400 record. After the defeat by McKay, Johnson would not lose another 400 final for eight years, a streak of 57 victories.

Outdoors, Johnson continued his series of sizzling
performances – before injury struck for a third consecutive
year. After a wind-aided 20.06 200 at the Texas Quadrangular
and a 43.8 relay leg at Kingston, Jamaica, the jinxed Johnson
was sidelined with a pulled hamstring. Despite the injury, Johnson
tried competing at the NCAA Outdoor Championships, but it was
a futile attempt. He ran 22.03 and finished fifth and last in his
200 heat. Michael ran one more race during the summer,
a 200 at Budapest, Hungary, and again he was fifth.

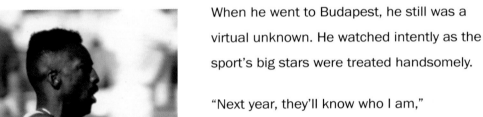

When he went to Budapest, he still was a
virtual unknown. He watched intently as the
sport's big stars were treated handsomely.

"Next year, they'll know who I am,"
he said to a friend.

They sure would.

He also told his sister Regina, "I am going to do
things that have never been done."

How prophetic.

In 1990, Johnson was injury free for the first time in his collegiate career – thanks to an intensive program of weight lifting and stretching specially designed to alleviate the stress on his tender hamstrings. What a spectacular season he had.

Not counting relays, he ran 21 races and won 20. His only defeat was by Leroy Burrell of the University of Houston at the Southwest Conference Outdoor Championships – and it took the fastest 200 in history to beat him. Burrell, who later became the world record-holder at 100 meters, ran a wind-aided 19.61 to Johnson's 19.91.

After that, Johnson reeled off 14 consecutive victories, including 200 wins at the NCAA Championships, the USA Championships, the Goodwill Games and the Grand Prix Final. The NCAA title began a two-year streak of 32 straight victories. Along the way that year, he cracked 20 seconds three times, with 19.90 at the national championships, 19.85 at Edinburgh and 19.88 at altitude in Sestriere, Italy.

U.S. CHAMPION | *400 meters (1993, 1995, 1996, 2000)*

400

In the 400, he beat world record-holder Butch Reynolds at Cologne, Germany, and lowered his personal best to 44.21. He also ran several sparkling relay legs, including 43.5 and 43.6.

"I'm starting to like the 400 more and more," Michael said. "I think I can do some great things in it."

That sensational senior season earned him No. 1 world rankings in the 200 and 400 – the first time any athlete had achieved that double – and he was chosen track and field's athlete of the year.

If Michael had not had such a brilliant season, he might not be in track and field now. "I probably would have used my degree [in marketing, from Baylor] and gone into business," he said. "I decided my last [senior] year was going to be a make-or-break year for me. The injuries discouraged me for a while, but I knew the potential was there, so I overruled them."

" After 200 meters, Michael just took off.
He ran away from us.

It was the most incredible thing I've ever seen.

If somebody had been with him, he could have run 42.6."

AMERICAN ANTONIO PETTIGREW, AFTER BEING BEATEN BY JOHNSON'S WORLD RECORD 43.18 AT THE 1999 WORLD CHAMPIONSHIPS IN SEVILLE, SPAIN

Criticism of Johnson's running form continued unabated, even though he was the world's best long sprinter at the tender age of 23. The critics still couldn't understand how he could run so fast with such rigid form. All they had to do was look at the results.

"I've always run my own way," Johnson said. "I hardly think anyone would dare suggest my style is all that wrong."

Track Tips for
Young Runners:
KEEP A DAILY LOG

KEEP A LOG OR RECORD OF YOUR DAILY ACHIEVEMENTS, YOUR TRAINING AND YOUR PROGRESS. THAT WILL SHOW HOW FAR YOU'VE GONE AND HOW MUCH FARTHER YOU HAVE TO GO. "A LOG PROVIDES TWO NECESSARY THINGS FOR SELF-DISCIPLINE: MOTIVATION AND HABIT," JOHNSON SAID. "RECORDING YOUR PROGRESS IN WRITING KEEPS YOU FOCUSED."

#4

No one should have, but they did.

"My advice is that everyone should run in the way that feels most natural for him or her," Michael said. "I've never tried to imitate anyone else, and if you want to be best you have to go your own way."

There was no question now that the mentally and physically rejuvenated Johnson wanted to be the best, and he already was, according to the rankings. The next steps were to win a world championship and to win an Olympic gold medal.

What made him No. 1 was his running style, even if it was unusual. His physique — a muscular 6-foot-1, about 180 pounds — was not along the lines of such great long sprinters of the past as Tommie Smith and Henry Carr.

Johnson's stride was about seven feet, nearly two feet shorter than Smith's remarkable high-kicking feet that would gobble up ground with incredible speed. Michael did not run in the classic, high-knee style, but he had amazing turnover and undeniable speed, and Hart was not going to tamper with it.

Track Tips for
Young Runners:
SET INTERIM GOALS

DREAM SMALL. THINK IN SMALL INCREMENTS. DON'T TRY TO DO TOO MUCH TOO FAST. "SHORT-TERM GOALS ARE THE ONLY RELIABLE PATH," JOHNSON SAID.

#5

"I have more speed than anybody I know," Johnson said, without trying to sound boastful. "I don't even have to work on speed ... What I have to work on is endurance ... I can work on my speed any time that I know I'm going into a 200-meter race that's going to be really hot. Other than that, the endurance work that I'm doing for the 400 meters will carry me over. The endurance aspect of my 200 meters and my 400 meters, plus the natural speed that I have, is enough to get me through."

" He's done things in a way unlike anyone else.

He'll go down as one of the all-time greats in the sport."

LEROY BURRELL, FORMER WORLD RECORD-HOLDER AT 100 METERS
AND NOW COACH AT THE UNIVERSITY OF HOUSTON

Ralph Mann, a former Olympic 400-meter hurdler and a biomechanical expert, analyzed Johnson's form and found it perfect. Mann formulated a model for the ideal 200, which revealed that rapidity of stride turnover was more important than stride length. He determined that Michael's was the most efficient in the world because his feet stayed on the ground for only .08 seconds. Good sprinters are said to remain in contact with the ground for .10 seconds, elite sprinters for .09 seconds.

"Because his stride doesn't use up as much energy, he can sprint at the end," Coach Hart said. "He is the only one who can keep his stride for an entire 400 because he runs so relaxed. Throw all the other models away for sprinting. Michael is the model."

With that endorsement and his college degree in hand, Michael was ready to become a professional. He wanted to make a comfortable living for himself and his family, and track was his outlet. His venture into the business world would have to wait.

WORLD OUTDOOR CHAMPION | 200 meters (1991, 1995)

WHEN JOHNSON LAUNCHED HIS PRO CAREER IN THE SUMMER OF 1990,

HIS APPEARANCE FEE ROSE RAPIDLY AS HIS VICTORIES MOUNTED.

"I'M NOT A SCHOOLKID ANYMORE, AND THIS IS NOT A HOBBY," HE SAID.

"IT'S A CAREER ... IN COLLEGE, IT WAS A HOBBY. THIS IS DEFINITELY

MORE FUN. BUT AS MUCH AS I LOVE THE SPORT ... IF IT WASN'T

MAKING ME MONEY AND PAYING MY BILLS, I WOULD HAVE TO DO

SOMETHING ELSE."

RANK | nine times No. 1 in world, 400 meters

He did not have to worry about doing anything else.

He was the best at what he did, and he was making lots of money.

"I'm competing to guarantee myself a harmonious, smooth-running

life after my career," Johnson said. "I'm competing to give myself security ..."

Security was assured.

If 1990 was an outstanding year, 1991 was even better.

Michael was undefeated in 15 200s and 10 400s. He ran a

legal 20.06 or better for the 200 nine times (nobody else did it

even once), and he ran the two fastest 400 times of the year

(a career-best 44.17 and 44.22). He also broke his world indoor

record in the 200 by .04 seconds, with a 20.55 in his first

meet of the year at Lievin, France. Highlighting the season

were victories in the 200 at the World Championships –

his first world title and the Grand Prix Final.

At the Worlds Championships in Tokyo, he won by more than three meters and was timed in a championship record 20.01 while running into an 8-1/2-mile per hour headwind.

Before settling into the starting blocks, Johnson had told himself, "Run the curve as hard as you can, then bring it home."

It might have been the fastest curve run until then.

His margin of victory (.33 seconds) was the biggest in a World Championship or Olympic 200 final since Jesse Owens won at the Berlin Games in 1936. Somehow, Johnson's name kept being linked with Owens. When Michael's running style was criticized, Coach Hart countered by saying that more people should run like Johnson, because he ran like Owens. Johnson winced at the analogy. "That's a lot of pressure," he said, but he learned to let it drive him.

Had the wind not been so fierce in that World Championship 200, Johnson might have broken the world record of 19.72 held by Italy's Pietro Mennea since 1979.

"That was the first time I honestly went for the world record," Johnson said. "But I have to be patient as far as the record is concerned. You have to have perfect conditions and you have to have it in your mind that you're going to go for it. You have to know that it's a fast track or it's a high profile meet, or something that's going to propel you to go that fast.

"Otherwise, you can't say, 'I'm going to go for it today.'"

Johnson was confident that he eventually would break the 200 record – plus the 400 record.

"I think I'm capable of breaking the world record at both distances," he said dispassionately.

Michael capped his 200 season with four straight races under 20.00 – 19.98, 19.89, 19.94 and 19.88. Those four and his 44.22 for 400 meters came within a two-week period in Europe, the greatest stretch of long sprinting in history until that point.

Earlier, in the 44.17 at Lausanne, Switzerland, the redoubtable Johnson had beaten a field that included 1988 Olympic gold medalist Steve Lewis, 1988 Olympic bronze medalist Danny Everett, 1991 world champion-to-be Antonio Pettigrew and Cuba's Roberto Hernandez, one of the world's fastest 400-meter runners.

1995 U.S. OUTDOOR CHAMPIONSHIPS | 200-400 double, first since 1899

Again Johnson was ranked No. 1 in the world in both the 200 and 400. Until Michael came along, no one in the world had achieved that honor, and now he had done it twice in a row.

The 1992 season got off to a rousing start with three victories in the 200 and two in the 400 before Johnson finally lost. His outdoor winning streak in the 200 was snapped at 32 finals when he finished second to Frank Fredericks of Namibia at the Golden Gala meet in Rome. Johnson's time of 20.25 was his slowest in nearly a year.

That was Michael's final race before the Olympic trials, and he knew he had a lot of work to do. Dedicated as usual to preparing in a businesslike fashion, he was ready. He breezed through the first-round heats and quarterfinals before easing up and finishing second to Mike Marsh in the semifinals. Marsh, the eventual 1992 Olympic champion, was a very formidable opponent, but Johnson beat him, along with Carl Lewis, Leroy Burrell and Dennis Mitchell, in the final in 19.79, a career-best and a trials record, breaking the mark of 19.84 set by Lewis in 1984. What was more amazing was that he ran that time out of lane eight, one of the most disadvantageous spots on the track and the first time Johnson had run from that position.

Before the race, Johnson zeroed in on each opponent.

Track Tips for
Young Runners:
SLACKING OFF

DON'T SLACK OFF IN YOUR TRAINING. IF YOU'RE SCHEDULED TO DO TWO HOURS EACH DAY, DO TWO HOURS, NOT A MINUTE LESS. IF YOU SHORTCHANGE YOURSELF, THAT CAN ONLY LEAD TO CUTTING CORNERS ON OTHER DAYS, NOT A GOOD SIGN OF SELF-DISCIPLINE.

"I glowered from under a tense brow at every other runner on the track that day, stared them down and sized them up," Michael wrote in his book, *Slaying the Dragon.* "I was in something my coach and I would later call the zone – the Danger Zone – because that day everyone on the track was in my sights, in my zone, in imminent danger. That day, I found a place to go where I felt the power of competition and the singular strength of my own commitment. To this day, it is the most outstanding example of focus and determination that I can remember, and it is the model for the mental state I try to use now when I run."

With such a stunning victory over many of the world's best 200-meter runners, Johnson was firmly established as the Olympic favorite.

Before the Games, which were five weeks away, Johnson would run three races in Europe to help keep him sharp for Barcelona. He never overraced; he just liked to run often enough to keep his competitive edge.

In his first race, a 200, he beat a strong international field that included Olapade Adeniken of Nigeria, Linford Christie and John Regis of Britain and Robson da Silva of Brazil in 20.10. He followed that with his 23rd consecutive victory in the 400, breaking 44 seconds for the first time, with 43.98 at London, leaving Steve Lewis, Antonio Pettigrew, Andrew Valmon and Brits Roger Black and Derek Redmond far back.

WORLD INDOOR RECORD | 400 meters: 44.63

The final tuneup was a 19.91 200 victory
at Salamanca, Spain – and that proved disastrous.

With three weeks remaining before the Olympics, Johnson had hoped to train
and fine-tune back in Dallas for an all-out assault on the gold medal. He couldn't
even work out for two weeks. A case of food poisoning wrecked his body and his
workout schedule. By the time he resumed workouts a week before the Games,
he had lost 10 pounds and was very weak. As the Olympics neared, though,
he felt he was regaining his strength and could win the gold medal.

His hopes were quickly dashed. He barely won his first-round heat and
finished second in the quarterfinals even while running full blast.
He knew that something was drastically wrong. Recovery was not
as swift as he had thought. Would he even make the final?

No way.

In the semifinals, Johnson was slow
out of the blocks and found himself
in the uncharacteristic position of
chasing the other runners instead of
them pursuing him. He never did catch
up and finished sixth, the worst of his
career in any 200 or 400. He was
heartbroken. Here was the top 200 meter
runner in the world for the past three
years and the prohibitive Olympic favorite
not even qualifying for the final.

Devastated, Michael was ready to leave Barcelona and return home, skipping an opportunity to run on the 1,600-meter relay team. He felt like a fighter who had been punched in the stomach and all the air had come out of him. His ego also was deflated. He knew he was the best in the world and if he couldn't compete at his peak, he didn't want to run at all.

His family and Coach Hart came to the rescue. They convinced him to stay and run the relay. Their advice was rewarded. Even though Johnson ran the slowest leg on the relay, the team won easily and Michael had his first Olympic gold medal. He would cherish it but would have to wait four more years for an individual gold medal. His post-Olympic malaise lasted only a short time. After realizing there was nothing he could have done to control what had happened, he resumed his normal lifestyle.

There were more races to win, more records to set and more titles to gain.

The 1992 off-season seemed a little longer than usual, but after some reflection, Michael was anxious to begin competing again. His goal for 1993 was to win the 400 at the World Championships.

To help realize that quest, he opened the season by running four indoor races in Europe and winning them all. He then won his only outdoor race before the USA Championships – the meet that would determine the American team for the World Championships at Stuttgart, Germany. In the final at the national championships, Johnson was awesome. Primed as never before, he won in a career-best 43.74, beating world record-holder Butch Reynolds, 1992 Olympic gold medalist Quincy Watts, Valmon, Pettigrew and Derek Mills.

This time, he ran two tuneup races in Europe, both victories, before the World Championships. He also watched what he ate, making certain there would be no recurrence of food poisoning. There wasn't, and he was psyched for the World Championships. This time, he was able to show his extraordinary speed, and it resulted in a winning effort of 43.65, another personal best, and the third-fastest 400 ever. Capping his World Championship performance, Johnson anchored the U.S. 1,600-meter relay team to victory in a world record 2:54.29, with a blazing anchor leg of 42.93.

He finished the season with four more victories in the 400, extending his winning streak to 35.

His concentration on the 400 had affected his 200. He lost four 200s, three to Fredericks, one in the Grand Prix Final, and one to Carl Lewis.

Nineteen-ninety-four was an "off" year for track and field. There were no Olympic Games and no World Championships. That enabled Johnson to run some 100-meter races just to see how he would fare. The answer was not well — he won only one of a handful of races. Still, there was some consolation. He lowered his personal best from 10.12 to 10.09. He also won the Goodwill Games 200, beating Fredericks, Marsh and Regis at St. Petersburg, Russia, in 20.10, after having lost to Fredericks twice.

Track Tips for
Young Runners:
MAKING ADJUSTMENTS

DON'T BE AFRAID TO REASSESS YOUR TRAINING SCHEDULE AT CERTAIN TIMES. CHECK TO SEE IF YOU'RE HEADED IN THE RIGHT DIRECTION. DECIDE IF YOU NEED TO MAKE ADJUSTMENTS, IF YOUR GOALS STILL ARE REALISTIC, IF YOU HAVEN'T OVERESTIMATED OR UNDERESTIMATED YOUR ABILITY.

The following year brought new goals — become the first runner in the 20th century to win the 200 and 400 double at the USA Championships, then become the first to sweep both events at the World Championships. If he could accomplish that herculean feat, he would lobby the International Amateur Athletic Federation, the sport's world-governing body, to change the 1996 Olympic schedule, allowing him to try and become the first man to win that double at the Olympic Games. This was Johnson's biggest challenge ever. He had the full support of his family and coach.

OLYMPIC GOLD MEDAL | 1,600-meter relay (1992)

THE 1995 SEASON BEGAN IN DAZZLING FASHION. JOHNSON SMASHED THE WORLD INDOOR RECORD IN THE 400 TWICE, FIRST WITH 44.97 AT RENO, NEVADA, THEN THREE WEEKS LATER WITH 44.63 AT THE USA CHAMPIONSHIPS IN ATLANTA. AFTER A FEW TUNEUP RACES OUTDOORS, HE WAS SET FOR HIS RARE DOUBLE AT THE NATIONAL CHAMPIONSHIPS AT STEAMY SACRAMENTO, CALIFORNIA. HE WOULD HAVE TO RUN SIX RACES IN FIVE DAYS. NO PROBLEM.

200-400

WORLD CHAMPIONSHIPS | only man to win 200-400 double (1995)

He conserved his energy in the quarterfinals and semifinals of the 400, his first event, then blasted out in the final and won in 43.66, only .01 second off his lifetime best. Michael followed the same pattern in the 200. In the quarterfinals and semifinals, he coasted, then went all out in the final and won in a wind-aided 19.83. No one had swept these two events at the nationals since 1899.

"I've always said there are two races with that guy [Johnson] in the race.

People who say they are going to beat Michael Johnson are idiots.

The only way to beat Michael is to run a perfect race and have him make a mistake, but he doesn't make mistakes."

ROGER BLACK OF BRITAIN, THE SILVER MEDALIST BEHIND JOHNSON IN THE 400 METERS AT THE 1996 OLYMPIC GAMES

Next was the World Championships at Göteborg, Sweden. This would be a much bigger test. Here, Johnson would face the best in the world and he would have to run eight races, four in each event. Again, he gauged his opposition perfectly. He ran only fast enough to win his first three heats in the 400, then unleashed a scorching 43.39 – the second-fastest ever and only .10 seconds off the world record – in the final.

His biggest concern now was that switching from the 400 to the 200 so quickly might lead to mistakes. Not to worry.

Johnson again began with a relatively slow time in winning his opening 200, then smartly reduced his times in the quarterfinals and semifinals before reeling off a sensational 19.79 – matching his career best and only .07 seconds off the world record – in winning the final. His winning margin over Fredericks was .33 seconds, matching his 1991 victory. Johnson now had won four individual world titles by the largest margin at a major championship since electronic timing began at the 1952 Olympics.

Michael had made his point to the IAAF. Change the schedule for Atlanta and I'll show you I can do the same thing. The schedule-makers were reluctant at first, but slowly began to bend, indicating there was a possibility they might yield.

Primo Nebiolo, the late IAAF president, said he thought Johnson could handle the 200-meter semifinal and the 400 final on the same day. "If he wants to run backwards, he could still do it," Nebiolo said.

Despite the IAAF's lack of speed, Johnson wasn't taking any chances. He thought the organization might eventually go over to his side, so he began training harder than ever.

"I'd learned quite a bit from my two attempts running the double," he said. "I knew I needed to be stronger, so I increased my weight-room workouts and put another 10 pounds on my frame. I'd never weighed more than 175 pounds, but now I was 185 and I had successfully added strength and stamina without losing speed."

Finally, in March 1996, the IAAF relented. It would yield to Johnson's request and revise the schedule, giving him the opportunity he was seeking.

Now came the pressure. Could he do it? Would he fail like at Barcelona? Was he asking too much of himself in such a high-profile arena and setting himself up for ridicule? Would he make the IAAF look foolish?

The questions were innumerable, the answers uncertain.

Johnson began putting replies to those queries at the Olympic trials in Atlanta.

After finishing second in each of his first three rounds of the 400, when he let other runners beat him, Johnson blistered the new Atlanta track in the final, winning in 43.44, the third-fastest time ever. He kept coming close to Reynolds' world-record 43.29, but just falling short.

Johnson didn't take any chances in the 200. He won each of his heats, running a wind-aided 19.70 – the second-fastest under any conditions – in the semifinals, then shattered the world record in winning the final at 19.66 for his 21st consecutive triumph. Everything was going according to plan, just the way Johnson liked.

With the trials over, the pressure increased, from the media and commercial sponsors. Everyone wanted a piece of Johnson. Michael added to the electric atmosphere by saying, "What this means is history. There are two household names in the history of track and field – Jesse Owens and Carl Lewis. I'm in position to be the third."

"I just wish more people still thought I couldn't do it,"
he added. "The higher the stakes, the better I am."

Shortly afterward, Johnson received a letter from Jesse Owens'
widow, Ruth, wishing him luck and saying Michael reminded her
of her late husband in the way he ran and the manner he carried
himself off the track. Johnson took that letter with him to Atlanta.

"It was perhaps the greatest accomplishment in the sport."

ERV HUNT, COACH OF THE 1996 U.S. OLYMPIC MEN'S TRACK TEAM,
AFTER JOHNSON'S STUNNING, RECORD-BREAKING PERFORMANCE
IN THE 200 AT THE ATLANTA GAMES

Before the Games, Michael ran three races in Europe. He easily won the first, with
43.66 for 400 meters at Lausanne, Switzerland. Next was a 200 at Oslo, Norway, and
Johnson was beaten by his old nemesis, Fredericks, 19.83 to 19.85. Two days later, he
won a 200 at Stockholm, Sweden, in 19.77, but that loss to Fredericks raised doubts
about Johnson's ability to sweep the 200 and 400 at Atlanta. Suddenly, Fredericks was
made the 200 favorite. Michael wasn't concerned. He realized he had made a mental
mistake at the start of the Oslo race and he wouldn't repeat it. Fredericks' attitude also
helped. He said Johnson should be the favorite, not he. It was an attempt to deflect the
pressure back to Johnson, but Michael looked at it as Fredericks taking a
negative attitude toward his own chances, a cardinal sin.

Always be positive was Johnson's philosophy,
or else you're beating yourself.

At last, the Olympics arrived, and it was time for the 400, the first of Michael's two finals. He easily made it through the prelims, and now the big moment was at hand ... the chance for his first individual Olympic gold medal. With 80,000 screaming fans in attendance, Johnson burst from the blocks. Propelled by his dream of double Olympic gold, he flashed across the finish line in 43.49, another tantalizing near-miss at Reynolds' record, but records were unimportant now. Johnson had won and he began celebrating, taking a victory lap with the American flag wrapped around him and posing for pictures with a wide-eyed smile. The usually unflappable Johnson had come unwrapped. He stopped to give his golden shoes to his parents. He was No. 1 and so were they. When the national anthem played, he cried.

The celebrating didn't last long. Johnson had to get focused on the 200. After winning his first two heats, Michael was hurting. He had a sore left Achilles tendon, an ailing tendon behind his left knee and a sacroiliac joint that needed constant adjustment. Yet his confidence never wavered. He would block out the pain, and he did in winning his semifinal heat. Now, it was time for the biggest race of his life.

Crouched in the blocks, with a gold chain around his neck and his lightweight golden shoes snug on his feet, Michael was tense but focused. When the gun exploded, so did Johnson. Despite a stumble on his third step, he caught Fredericks at 80 meters. From there to the finish line, it was Johnson against the clock.

Johnson won!

He didn't just beat Fredericks and the others, he beat them with an astonishing time of 19.32! A world record by .34 seconds! Unheard of in such a short race.

The dream had been fulfilled, the skeptics quieted.

Johnson's emotions all came flowing out. He was soaking up the moment, enjoying the unprecedented accomplishment ... an Olympic double, a world record. This was the pinnacle of his career. There was the victory lap with the American flag, the pictures alongside the clock on the field showing his time, the hugs and kisses from family and friends, and the tears.

His image was completely wrong, Johnson insisted.
He wanted to break through the facade.

"I want to correct the image people have of me," he said. "I'm serious about running, but I also like to joke and laugh and have a lot of fun."

Johnson was thoroughly enjoying himself and thoroughly exhausted.
So tired that he couldn't run on the relay team.

Asked how it felt to go faster than any man had gone before, Johnson said, "It was like the first time I went down the hill at the end of our street in the go-cart my father made for me."

There was no doubt he was the world's No. 1 track and field athlete, and he wanted to retain that title.

"Being ranked No. 1 in the world is the main priority," he said as the 1997 season approached. "You don't want to be second in your event. I want to go to the World Championships and win. I want to go to the Olympics and win. I want to go to the [150-meter] match race against [Olympic 100-meter champion] Donovan Bailey and win. I don't want to get silver. The fear of being second keeps it exciting. Every race is exciting. It's a job and the objective is to win, to be the best at what you do.

"Nothing could top Atlanta. That was overwhelming. That week or 1-1/2 weeks was the realization of my dreams coming true. It excites me to do things no one else has done. That's part of what drives me. The 19.32 is the glaring moment that stands out and it will probably define my career."

In 1997, Johnson experienced physical problems and his racing was limited. He injured his right quadricep in his confrontation with Bailey. Then, his left leg was found to be one-third weaker and one-third slower in reaction time than his right. An imbalance in Johnson's hips was putting extra stress on the left leg.

"It was like running with a flat tire," Hart said.

Flat tire or not, Johnson got pumped up enough to win another 400-meter world title at Athens, Greece – again with the help of the IAAF and without having run a race for about 1-1/2 months. The world body allowed Johnson – and other defending world champions – to compete even though he had not qualified for the U.S. team, giving him a wild-card entry.

Track Tips for
Young Runners:
LOSING GRACEFULLY

LEARN TO LOSE GRACEFULLY.
"YOU WILL BE REMEMBERED BY THE WAY YOU WIN AND LOSE, BY YOUR GREATEST ACHIEVEMENTS AND YOUR WORST FAILURES," JOHNSON SAID. "LEARN THE DIFFERENCE BETWEEN GLOATING AND CELEBRATING, BETWEEN MOPING AND MOURNING."

#8

"You had to be standing behind Michael at the World Championships to see how much he was hurting," Hart said. "His left leg, he had no control.

"He's always been able to push another button. He has the ability in a big race to separate himself. He has a God-given talent to reach down and get to another level."

1996

The injuries were disconcerting to Johnson. He didn't
know whether he was going to get hurt when he trained.
Chiropractic treatments helped ease the pain.

Less than four weeks after being humiliated by Bailey, Johnson tried
returning to competition. It was an unwise decision. In a 400 race at Paris,
he had his eight-year, 58-race winning streak ended, finishing a dismal fifth.

"It just proves that no one
is superhuman," Britain's Roger Black
said. "I thought he was, but he's not.
He's like the rest of us."

The hamstring and hip injuries
continued to plague Johnson
during 1998, undercutting his season.
The biggest race he won that year
was the Goodwill Games 400 at
Uniondale, New York.

In 1999, Johnson was scheduled to have 200 showdowns with 100-meter
world record-holder Maurice Greene at the U.S. Pro Championships in
Uniondale and the USA Championships at Eugene, Oregon. They never materialized.
Johnson missed the Pro Championships because of the death of his grandmother.
A right quadriceps injury forced him to withdraw just before the national
championships. Greene contended that Johnson was ducking him. Hart insisted
that Johnson was hurt at Eugene and was not in the habit of ducking anyone.

Johnson had brought his wife Kerry and his brother and sister to Eugene to watch him run, so pulling out was devastating.

About a week after the injury, Johnson won a 400 at Lausanne in 43.92; five days later, he ran a 19.93 200 at Rome, becoming the first runner to run a sub-20 and sub-44 in the same week. Later at a meet in Stockholm, Sweden, he pulled up after 150 meters of a 400. He then came back home and met with Hart. Johnson was tired of the injuries and of the criticism, and claimed running wasn't fun any more.

At that point, in early August, Johnson considered retiring. He drove from his home in Dallas to Waco and met with Hart.

"When he walked into my office that day, Michael was at a lower point, physically and mentally, than I'd ever seen him," Hart said. "He was very, very down."

Hart reminded Michael that his goal for the year was to break the 400 record, and there still was time. Johnson listened and reconsidered. With newfound determination, he resumed serious workouts. The training went so well that Hart found it "scary" because Michael was running 400s in 42.6 in 100-degree heat.

At Seville, Spain, he gave an indication that he could break the record when he ran 43.95 in the semifinals while shutting down 100 meters from the finish. He lived up to expectations. In the final, Johnson finally caught up and passed Reynolds' record, running 43.18, for his fourth consecutive 400 world title. Johnson helped close the championships by anchoring the U.S. relay team to a gold medal, his ninth at the World Championships, surpassing the record of eight by Carl Lewis.

That brought him into 2000 with high expectations and exuberance, and plans for another Olympic double. He was mentally rejuvenated after the World Championships.

"A race with seven other guys is all I need to get excited about going to the track every day," he said.

Especially with the Olympics coming up.

"There's nothing like winning an Olympic gold medal," Johnson said. "The opportunity will be there to run 42 [in the 400]. I think I'm capable of running that. I don't think much about records in the 200 anymore. I don't think I broke the 400 by enough. I think I can do better."

He also is keenly aware that no man has repeated in the Olympic 200 or 400.

"I feel great about my chances of winning both again," Michael said. "There's a lot of pressure, even if you're doing it for the first time. The advantage I'll have is that I've done it before."

"The only enemy he has is injuries," Hart said.

With all of Johnson's success, he has not forgotten his family. He bought his parents a new home in a Dallas suburb. He's financially helped his siblings, who gave him spending money in college. And he's providing for his wife and son, Sebastian, born in 2000.

MICHAEL JOHNSON VS. DONOVAN BAILEY
the match race

One of the few daunting moments in Johnson's illustrious track career was his 1997 150-meter match race against Donovan Bailey of Canada. Prior to their $2 million showdown at SkyDome in Toronto, the two were verbally sparring like heavyweight fighters hyping a championship match. Actually, the race was for an unofficial title – "The World's Fastest Human."

Johnson had set the world 200-meter record of 19.32 seconds at the 1996 Olympics, five days after Bailey broke the world 100-meter record, running 9.84 at the Atlanta Games.

Each was convinced he was the world's fastest man and didn't have to beat the other to prove it.

"Why would I need bragging rights over Donovan Bailey?" Johnson said. "I have two gold medals, two world records, Olympic history, I have a 58-race win streak and I haven't lost in the 400 meters since 1989. I have more sub-20 second 200s than anyone else in the world and I'm better known than any other sprinter in the world at this point."

Bailey was just as cocky.

"I'm naturally faster," he said. "The only thing I have to worry about – if I have to worry about anything – is the extra 50 meters. If I relax and breathe properly, this will be a cakewalk."

Each participant was guaranteed $500,000, and the winner would earn $1 million.

Johnson was so certain of victory, he said he would put the entire prize on the line. Bailey was more cautious. "Why should I do that?" he said. "This is my job."

Johnson, however, was excited about the rarely contested match race.

"It's a great event for the sport," he said. "I'm doing it because I stand to make a fairly large amount of money. I'm a pro athlete. That's what I do, and it's great entertainment for the fans.

"I don't feel I have any score to settle with Donovan Bailey, because he and I are not really competitors in regular track and field events. [Bailey sticks to the 100, while Johnson runs the 200 and 400.] As far as who's the fastest man in the world is concerned, whichever one of us wins the race will certainly get to hold that title, and that's great. A lot of people already are calling me the fastest man in the world, and a lot of people are calling him that as well. You're going to have someone say Carl Lewis is the fastest man in the world, or something crazy like that ... I don't think this race is going to change their minds. The debate is great for track and field, especially if it gets them excited and talking

about something other than world records."

Johnson said he hoped the idea of made-for-TV events catches on in track because "if you just show normal track meets, it's hard to bring in new fans – they've seen it before."

When the two combatants finally got onto the track together – the first time either ever had competed at 150 meters – the race was over less than halfway from the start. That's because Johnson pulled up after 70 meters with a strained left hamstring.

Bailey, true to his boast of being the winner in a "cakewalk," and flushed with success, called Johnson a "coward" and a "chicken" for not finishing. He claimed Johnson faked his injury, an accusation that irritated Michael.

"The worst thing that could have happened, happened," Brad Hunt, Johnson's agent, said. "It's unfortunate the outcome was as bad as it could have been."

Johnson was perturbed by Bailey's continual backbiting after the race, but said he didn't regret competing despite sustaining the injury. He tried displaying a lot more class and dignity than the Canadian.

"It shows a lot about the kind of person he is and I'm not going to address this," Michael said.

"I've always respected Donovan as an athlete."

The following day the contrite Bailey apologized.

"I have tremendous respect for Michael's ability," the Canadian said, "and I hope the injury ... is not season-threatening."

Clyde Hart, Johnson's coach, was "embarrassed" by the reaction of the fans at SkyDome.

"Michael's lying down getting treated, and we get water and things thrown at us," Hart said.

Johnson was downcast but philosophical.

"When you get injured, it's always disappointing," he said. "Every race, whether it's a victory, a loss or you get injured ... you've got to put it behind you. I have one injury and one loss in the last year. I wouldn't consider that a tough stretch."

Does he regret participating in this sloppily promoted but widely hyped event? "The answer is NO with a capital N and a capital O," Michael said. "How could I? How could I turn down the opportunity to run in what was the biggest race – other than the Olympic Games – I've ever run?"

Clyde Hart has been Michael Johnson's coach since 1986, and he is someone Michael trusts and respects. "I couldn't do it without him," Michael said. "We're a team – we're partners. Those gold medals and world records, they're mine and his. They're both of ours."

Johnson's loyalty is something that Hart admires and treasures. Michael gave his coach one shoe that he wore when he set the 200-meter world record at the 1996 Olympic trials and another shoe when he broke the record again at the Atlanta Games. "He has been a coach, a friend, a hero and a mentor," Johnson said. "He's just a great person." Hart answers questions about Johnson and the results and accomplishments the two have achieved.

HOW WOULD YOU ASSESS THE DEVELOPMENT OF MICHAEL'S CAREER?

"He has progressed the way you would have wanted. He's been very successful over a 14-year period."

HOW WOULD YOU DESCRIBE THE IMPACT HE HAS HAD ON THE SPORT?

"It's hard to diagnose what impact he's had. I had doubts he could do the double at the 1996 Olympics. He convinced me he could do it, so I said go ahead. He's very motivated and he's worked hard to achieve his goals. His work ethic is still there and his demeanor hasn't changed – it's probably gotten stronger. He's as easy to coach as anybody I've ever had. He's someone coaches dream about. He's willing to work hard because he knows that it's necessary to get good. There have been people with his ability, but he doesn't jeopardize his chances to get good."

WHAT WERE HIS MOTIVATIONS FOR CONTINUING WITH TRACK AND FIELD WHEN HE GRADUATED FROM BAYLOR?

"When he found out there was a chance to make a good living in track and field, he worked at it. In 1988, he went to Europe to experience some running and see the world. He saw people being driven around in limousines, staying in five-star hotels and making big money, and he went for that goal."

WHERE DO YOU THINK MICHAEL SHOULD RANK IN THE PANTHEON OF GREAT TRACK ATHLETES AND WHY?

"My first opinion would be to rank him No. 1, but I'm prejudiced. He has to be in the top three or five. What he's done, he's done so easily, and he's won by big margins. He's broken the oldest records in track and field. He didn't just break them by hundredths of seconds, but by large margins. He holds the 200, 300 and 400 world records. He has the three fastest 200s ever run. Jesse Owens' records and Bob Beamon's long jump probably are the two best track performances I know of. Michael surpassed Beamon because his record in the 200 was his eighth race of the Games. What hasn't he done?"

ABOUT CLYDE HART

CLYDE HART IS MORE THAN A TRACK COACH. HE IS A TRACK COACH WHO EMPHASIZES THE IMPORTANCE OF EDUCATION. THAT'S ONE OF THE REASONS MICHAEL JOHNSON CHOSE TO ATTEND BAYLOR UNIVERSITY — BECAUSE HART STRESSED EDUCATION ALONG WITH ATHLETICS.

TO BEST ILLUSTRATE HART'S COMMITMENT TO EDUCATION AND TO SHOW THE QUALITY OF HIS STUDENT ATHLETES, A RECENT NCAA REPORT NOTED THAT HIS COMBINED MEN'S AND WOMEN'S PROGRAMS HAD AN 89 PERCENT GRADUATION RATE. THE IMPORTANCE OF ACADEMICS CAN BE SEEN IN THE SUCCESS OF KARIN ERNSTROM, A SENIOR DISTANCE RUNNER ON THE 2000 TEAM. SHE BECAME A MEMBER OF PHI BETA KAPPA, THE FIRST BAYLOR ATHLETE TO ACHIEVE THAT DISTINCTION.

LIKE MICHAEL JOHNSON, THE 66-YEAR-OLD HART WAS A SPRINTER WHEN HE WAS YOUNGER, BUT UNLIKE MICHAEL

HE WAS A SHORT SPRINTER RATHER THAN A LONG SPRINTER. HIS BEST TIME FOR THE 100 WAS A WIND-AIDED 9.3 SECONDS — HE RAN A LEGAL 9.5 — AND FOR THE 200 20.6 AT THE 1956 KANSAS RELAYS. HE ALSO RAN ON A 400-METER RELAY TEAM THAT EQUALED THE WORLD RECORD OF 40.3.

HART'S UNDOING AS A RUNNER CAME WHEN HE FACED HALL OF FAMER BOBBY MORROW AT A MEET OF CHAMPIONS IN HOUSTON. MORROW WON THE 100 IN 10.3, WHILE HART WAS FIFTH IN 10.5. "I KNEW THEN I WASN'T READY FOR THOSE PEOPLE," HART SAID.

A 1956 BAYLOR GRADUATE, HART DIDN'T TRY FOR THE OLYMPIC TEAM THAT YEAR. "I DIDN'T HAVE THE CONFIDENCE I COULD DO IT," HE SAID, "SO I WENT TO WORK."

HART MIGHT HAVE GONE FARTHER AS A RUNNER HAD HE NOT TORN HIS RIGHT HAMSTRING AS A SOPHOMORE, AN INJURY THAT REQUIRED SURGICAL REATTACHMENT.

"AFTER THAT, I HAD TO BE CAREFUL OF MY SORE LEG," HE SAID.

HIS WORK EVENTUALLY TOOK HIM BACK TO BAYLOR, WHERE HE HAS BEEN COACHING FOR 37 YEARS. UNDER HIS DISTINGUISHED LEADERSHIP, THE BEARS HAVE CONSISTENTLY BEEN ONE OF THE NATION'S TOP TEAMS, BOTH IN INDIVIDUAL EVENTS AND IN RELAYS.

HART WAS CHOSEN SOUTHWEST CONFERENCE COACH OF THE YEAR FOUR TIMES (1981, 1984, 1989, 1996), NCAA INDOOR COACH OF THE YEAR TWICE (1989, 1996) AND U.S. OLYMPIC COMMITTEE TRACK COACH OF THE YEAR IN 1996. HART HAS COACHED EIGHT WORLD RECORD PERFORMANCES (SEVEN INDIVIDUAL, ONE RELAY) AND WAS SELECTED AN ASSISTANT COACH FOR THE U.S. OLYMPIC TEAM FOR THE 2000 GAMES.

HE HAS ONE OF THE MOST IMPORTANT ATTRIBUTES FOR A COACH: HE UNDERSTANDS HIS ATHLETES. THAT HAS EARNED HIM THEIR UTMOST RESPECT. THAT IS OF UTMOST IMPORTANCE TO A COACH.

TRAINING routine

A TYPICAL TRAINING WEEK FOR MICHAEL JOHNSON:

Like everything else Michael Johnson does, his training routine is well organized. He hardly ever deviates from his schedule, for fear that a misstep would disrupt his goals.

Johnson, who lives in Dallas, Texas, travels to Waco, Texas, on Mondays, Tuesdays and Wednesdays to work with Coach Hart. His total training time ranges from 12 to 15 hours a week, three hours a day in Waco and an hour or more a day in Dallas.

MONDAY
Johnson does about five or six 200s at near 26-second speed with a minute and a half rest in between. He also does a session in the weight room.

TUESDAY
Devoted to overdistance work, with runs longer than 400 meters. He does at least two hard repeats of 450 to 600 meters with 15-minute rests. He likes to come through the first 400 in 48 seconds and the second in 46.

WEDNESDAY
Another workout in the weight room, along with an under 400-meter session on the track. The runs consist of three or four 300s or 350s, depending on the time of year. He does not lift a lot of weight, but does high repetitions. He can bench press 300 pounds by the start of a season.

THURSDAY
If he is not competing on Saturday, the practice consists of six to eight 100s or so-called 60-40 sprints, meaning he sprints 60 meters, then glides for 40 meters. After each, he takes a short walk, then repeats that routine several times. If he is competing, the workout will be a short warmup.

FRIDAY
Rest.

SATURDAY
Competition.

SUNDAY
No workout.

If he has no Saturday race, the season determines his routine. So on Friday, he might work on his starts and run six 100s or run 10 100s, and on Saturday, he might practice his starts and run some 30s, 40s, 50s and 60s or he might run three 275s.

He doesn't miss training at home for more than three weeks. Thus, if he is competing in Europe, he won't stay more than three weeks, so he can return home.

On race days, he meets with Coach Hart early, and they discuss details, such as where Johnson will go between races if he is running more than once that day. Should he stay in the stadium or return to the warmup track? When should he begin his final warmup? He is at the track an hour before his race to begin warming up, a headset hooked over his ears, listening to rap music. The power of the music gets his adrenaline flowing. At the warmup area, he stretches, runs a few starts and focuses his mind completely on his technique. The routine is monotonously familiar, but it works. When he gets to the starting line, he is fully ready, mentally and physically. When the gun fires, he is off and running, prepared to run the race of his life.